POP CULTURE BIOS
ACTION MOVIE STARS

LIAM HEMSWORTH

THE HUNGER GAMES' STRONG SURVIV

JODY JENSEN SHAFFER

Lerner Publications Company
MINNEAPOLIS

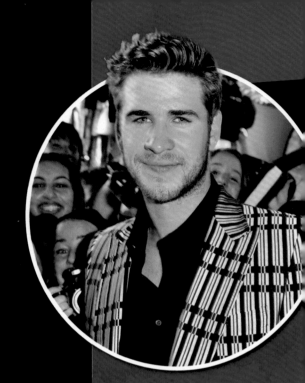

To DeeDee Jensen Gutshall and
Mark Jensen, the best sister
and brother ever

Lerner Publications Company
A division of Lerner Publishing Group, Inc.
241 First Avenue North
Minneapolis, MN 55401 U.S.A.

Website address: www.lernerbooks.com

Library of Congress Cataloging-in-Publication Data

Shaffer, Jody Jensen.
    Liam Hemsworth : the Hunger Games' Strong Survivor / by
Jody Jensen Shaffer.
      p.   cm. — (Pop culture bios: action movie stars)
    Includes bibliographical references and index.
    ISBN 978–1–4677–0742–8 (lib. bdg. : alk. paper)
    1. Hemsworth, Liam, 1990– —Juvenile literature.
    2. Actors—Australia—Biography—Juvenile literature. I. Title.
PN3018.H46S53 2013
791.4302'8092—dc23 [B]   2012013219

Manufactured in the United States of America
– PP – 12/31/12

INTRODUCTION PAGE **4**

CHAPTER ONE
GROWING UP DOWN UNDER
PAGE **6**

CHAPTER TWO
THE CITY OF ANGELS
PAGE **12**

CHAPTER THREE
THE HUNGER GAMES AND BEYOND
PAGE **20**

LIAM PICS!	28
SOURCE NOTES	30
MORE LIAM INFO	30
INDEX	31

INTRODUCTION

Liam (RIGHT), Jennifer Lawrence, and Josh Hutcherson promote *The Hunger Games* in March 2012.

Liam Hemsworth grabs his marker and smiles at the fan standing in front of him. She's been waiting hours for him to sign her favorite Liam poster. Her eyes well with tears. Her voice quavers. Liam doesn't mind. "It's very flattering to see how passionate [the fans] are," he says. Liam signs his name and hands the fan her poster. Then he greets his next admirer.

It's early March 2012. Liam, Jennifer Lawrence, and Josh Hutcherson are kicking off a string of mall tours with this stop at Westfield Century City mall in Los Angeles, California. They're promoting their movie *The Hunger Games*. One thousand screaming fans have come to meet them.

It took some getting used to at first—the attention, the crowds, the paparazzi. But that's what you get when you're the hottest thing in Hollywood and starring in the world's next blockbuster film. And if Liam's amazing looks and awesome talent are any indication, he'd better get really comfortable with scenes like this one in L.A.!

PAPARAZZI =
celebrity photographers

The Hemsworth family attends a movie premiere in 2011. FROM LEFT: Liam; Luke; Luke's wife, Samantha; Chris; Leonie; and Craig

CHAPTER ONE

GROWING UP DOWN UNDER

Liam was born in Melbourne, Australia

Liam Hemsworth was born on January 13, 1990, in Melbourne, Australia. Liam's mom, Leonie, is an English teacher. His dad, Craig, is a counselor. He's trained to help kids who are facing family problems. Liam has two older brothers, Luke and Chris. They also grew up to be actors.

Liam and his brothers had lots of free time when they were kids. They skateboarded, surfed, and raised pet guinea pigs. They also fought about who got to sit in the front seat of their family car! (Now Liam says his brothers are his "role models [and] best friends in the world.")

When Liam was eleven, his family moved from Melbourne to Phillip Island, about two hours away. They lived in a small house on a dirt road. Liam couldn't see a grocery store or a neighbor from his house.

Liam and his family moved to Phillip Island in 2001. Only about seven thousand people live on the island year-round.

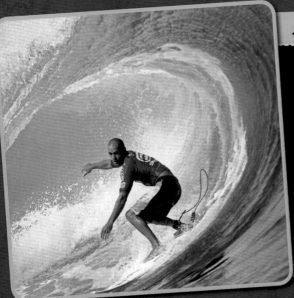

HANG TEN, DUDE!

Liam learned to surf when he was ten. Liam, his brothers, and their friends surfed every single day before and after school. They wanted to grow up to be like U.S. pro surfer Kelly Slater (LEFT), who's won ten world surfing titles.

Bitten

When Liam got to high school, he was bitten by the acting bug. By then, his brothers had found success acting on Australian TV shows. Liam thought he could do better! But beyond wanting to top his brothers, Liam had a sense that acting was what he really wanted to do with his life. So he took a drastic step. At sixteen, he got an agent and dropped out of high school. He signed up for an acting class. He began dedicating tons of time to trying out for TV and movie roles.

AGENT =
a person who tries
to find jobs for actor

Over the next three years, Liam's drastic step paid off. He landed many small parts on TV. He was making a

Liam's parents have always believed in their sons. When Liam announced that he wanted to quit high school, they were more than a little shocked! But they could see how much acting meant to him. They agreed that he could quit school if he made a commitment to work hard on his acting—and he did!

name for himself as an actor in Australia. When he wasn't acting, Liam worked for a company that installed floors in people's homes. He made fifteen dollars an hour.

Liam (RIGHT), at the age of sixteen, with his dad, mom, and brother Chris

From Small to Big Screen

In 2009 Liam got a big break: his first starring role in a movie. He played an American in the British film *Triangle*. Liam grew up watching American movies. But he needed help sounding like an American. So he hired an accent coach.

ACCENT COACH = a person who teaches others how to reduce their accent or to speak in a new accent

This pic is from the movie *Triangle*. Liam played Victor in the movie.

Liam also won a small part in the film *Knowing* with Nicolas Cage. But he was still looking for something bigger. He hoped to score a starring role in a major U.S. motion picture.

Expendable?

Before Liam's dream came true, he hit a rough patch. Around the time he got the part in *Knowing*, Liam taped a script reading for a film in the States. The film was called *The Expendables*. It would be directed by Sylvester Stallone.

Liam sent his taped script reading to Sylvester, and he offered Liam a role! Liam celebrated with his friends and packed his bags. Then things fell apart. *The Expendables'* script was rewritten. Liam's character was cut. He was shocked and embarrassed.

But Liam didn't suffer for long. Just a few hours (yes, *hours!*) later, director Kenneth Branagh called him. Kenneth asked Liam to try out for the lead role in his 2011 film *Thor*. It was just the kind of job that Liam had been hoping for. He was going stateside after all.

SCRIPT READING =

an informal performance in which actors sit around a table and read lines from a script

CHAPTER TWO

THE CITY OF ANGELS

When Liam (LEFT) first moved to Los Angeles, he moved in with Chris (RIGHT).

Liam and Miley Cyrus in a shot from *The Last Song*

Liam flew to Los Angeles in April 2009. He stayed with his brother Chris, who was now living in the United States. Right away, Liam started getting into character. He did everything he could to look the part of Thor (god of thunder and lightning). He ramped up his exercise routine to look more like the muscular god. He even sported a blond wig for the screen test.

SCREEN TEST =
a short movie filmed to
determine an actor's ability

This depiction of Thor, god of thunder and lightning, is from a Marvel comic book.

When Liam was a kid, he once dressed as a table tennis player for Halloween. The costume included a sweatband, a white tank top, and cute white "short shorts!"

Roller Coaster

While he waited to hear about *Thor*, Liam tried out for other roles. Then things fell apart for him a second time. Kenneth called. He'd given the role of Thor to someone else—and not just any "someone else." The role had gone to Liam's brother Chris! Liam was happy for Chris. But he was also very worried. Would he ever star in a major U.S. film?

Chris was a dead ringer for Thor, and the movie was a big success.

Liam's Dream Shot

Just when Liam started to panic about his career, something happened to show him that his hard work had all been worth it. Liam had been in Los Angeles for five weeks when he read the script for Nicholas Sparks's *The Last Song*. The Disney movie was about a piano player and a beach volleyball hunk. Liam tried out with the director and the producer. A week later, he was invited back to read with Miley Cyrus, the movie's star.

Liam hoped to play opposite Miley Cyrus (RIGHT) in the film based on the novel *The Last Song* by Nicholas Sparks (LEFT).

LIAM'S FAVES

Color: blue
Movies: *The Departed, Superbad, James Dean*
Actors: Matt Damon, George Clooney
Foods: sushi, anything fried
Sports: surfing, boxing

Liam cracked up when he saw a squirrel for the first time at a meetin at Disney. The only squirrel-like rode they have in Australia are in zoos.

Soon after that second reading, Disney announced that Liam had landed the part of volleyball player Will Blakelee! Liam would make his American movie debut opposite one of the world's most well-known people.

Sand 'n' Surf

Just a few weeks later, Liam was filming on Tybee Island near Savannah, Georgia. He had to learn to scuba dive for his role. He practiced in a tank in North Carolina. Then he swam with sharks and stingrays in an aquarium in Atlanta.

The aquarium rehearsals freaked Liam out a little. "The aquarium people said, 'You don't have to worry about the

Liam got to learn to scuba dive for

Miley has a laugh while shooting a scene for *The Last Song* with Liam.

sharks.... But the groupers have been known to bump people [and] bite them'" Liam recalled. Liam went on to describe how the groupers would "creep up on you with this big, stupid look on their face. They just look like they wanna headbutt you." It was unsettling even for a guy who's used to surfing in the ocean!

Liam also had to learn to play volleyball. He admits that he'd overstated his volleyball-playing skills when he first talked to the film's producers. Liam spent hours in the Georgia sun trying to get good. He had to wear wet-suit shoes on his feet to protect them from the hot sand.

THE PERFECT DATE

Liam's perfect date is a trip to the electronics store Best Buy. (He loves electronic gadgets.) Feed him sushi for dinner, show him an action flick, and he's yours!

Paparazzi

During the three months of filming, Liam learned what a huge star Miley was. (He had never heard Miley's music before.) He was shocked about all the attention she got. "The paparazzi is really crazy [in America]," he said. "I've never experienced anything like it. It is weird to have people follow you around all the time."

Liam and Miley grew to like each other during the filming. They began dating after filming ended. Miley took Liam to Nashville. She introduced him to her family and to country fried steak, a dish they don't serve in Australia. He loved it. When Liam returned to Los Angeles, he became a target for the paparazzi too. They took pictures of him wherever he went. They even flew to

Miley and Liam attempt (unsuccessfully) to avoid notice during an outing in L.A. in 2010.

Phillip Island when Liam went home for a visit.

Liam decided not to let the craziness get to him—a good idea in light of something he spotted in Los Angeles just before *The Last Song* came out. "I was driving down Sunset [Boulevard]," Liam remembered, "and there's this eight-story billboard with a poster for the movie on it. It's crazy to see my head that big!"

With his newfound fame, Liam was offered parts in several big films. But all of them fell through for one reason or another. Liam worked out his frustrations at a boxing gym. And he continued to audition.

Liam and Miley dazzle at the premiere of *The Last Song* in Hollywood, California, in 2010.

GUYS' NIGHT

Liam's ideal guys' night? Playing Xbox with his buddies and watching *Family Guy*. It doesn't take much to make Liam happy!

CHAPTER THREE

THE HUNGER GAMES AND BEYOND

Liam and Miley smile for the camera.

Then, in January 2011, Liam heard about the movie adaptation of Suzanne Collins's novel *The Hunger Games*. He wanted to be a part of it. He read all three books to get familiar with the story. Liam was gripped by the tale of children forced to fight to the death. And he loved the action.

The Call

When Liam read *The Hunger Games'* script, he thought he might like to play Peeta Mellark. Peeta was the son of a baker and one of the two male leads. Big bro Chris helped Liam rehearse. Chris read the lines of the female lead, Katniss Everdeen! Liam auditioned twice with the director. And then he waited.

In March Liam got a call that would change his life forever. Director Gary Ross offered Liam a role. He would play Gale Hawthorne, Katniss's best friend and the other male lead.

Liam poses with *The Hunger Games* author Suzanne Collins and director Gary Ross.

BIG Buzz

Hollywood began to buzz about the casting. Jennifer Lawrence had won the part of Katniss.

Josh Hutcherson would play Peeta. Insiders said *The Hunger Games* would make Liam, Jennifer, and Josh superstars. People compared the actors to Taylor Lautner, Robert Pattinson, and Kristen Stewart of the *Twilight* movies.

Jennifer Lawrence and Josh Hutcherson in February 2011

Artemis

Filming for *The Hunger Games* began in May 2011. The movie was shot in the mountains around Asheville and Hildebran, North Carolina. The producers called the project Artemis. They wanted to keep the location secret from reporters and fans.

Liam lost 20 pounds (9 kilograms) to play Gale. "I wanted to feel what it is to be hungry," he said. The characters of Gale, Peeta, and Katniss often have to go without food. One of the hardest scenes for Liam was the reaping scene. In this scene, the children of Panem—the fictional nation where the Hunger Games takes place—are gathered together to find out whether they will have to go to the games. In addition to being an emotionally hard scene, the weather was stifling. Extras fainted. Liam wasn't sure if he would make it through the filming.

EXTRA =
ordinary people hired to be in a movie. Extras don't usually have speaking parts.

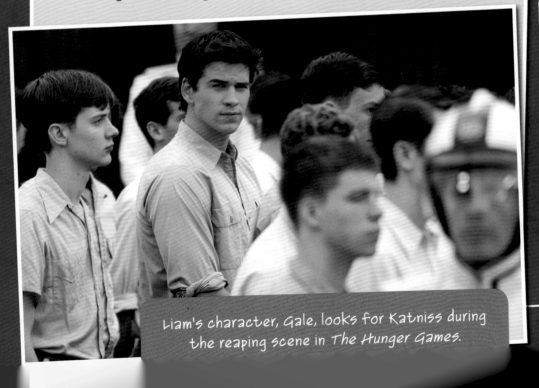

Liam's character, Gale, looks for Katniss during the reaping scene in *The Hunger Games*.

Fun and Games

But it wasn't all hard. Before Gary Ross yelled, "Action!" Jennifer would say something to make Liam crack up. "[She's] one of the most unpredictable people I've ever met!" laughed Liam.

While most of Liam's scenes were with Jennifer, he also had lots of fun with costar Josh Hutcherson. During a break in filming, Josh took Liam home to Kentucky. They ate White Castle burgers and shot hoops.

The Hunger Games premiered at Los Angeles's Nokia Theatre on March 12, 2012. Nearly five thousand fans lined up to get a peek at the movie's stars. Liam was calm and cool. He posed for pictures, did interviews, and signed his name. He was thrilled about how the movie turned out. "It's one of the most powerful films I've ever seen," he reflected. "It's really, really great."

BIG NEWS!

Liam and Miley dated on and off in 2010. In 2011 things got more serious between the pair. They seemed to be seeing each other exclusively. In 2012 things heated up even more when Liam proposed to Miley on May 31! The cute couple's pics were all over the news.

Liam helped design Miley's engagement ring with a Beverly Hills jeweler. The main diamond is antique, making it unique.

Blockbuster!

The rest of the world agreed. Thousands of people bought tickets early. Showings were sold out in theaters across America. And when *The Hunger Games* finally debuted throughout the country on March 23, 2012, it set records. The movie made $155 million in ticket sales its first weekend. It was the biggest weekend nonsequel opening ever and the third-biggest movie opening of all time!

Josh, Jennifer, and Liam stop for photos on the red carpet at the premiere of *The Hunger Games*.

Other Projects

Liam worked on other projects in 2011 too. He played the friend of a soldier who was dumped by his girlfriend in *AWOL*. The movie was filmed in Michigan. He also auditioned for—and got—the starring role in the 3-D adaptation of *Arabian Nights*. And he shot

The Expendables 2. Though his character was cut from the original *Expendables* in 2009, Sylvester Stallone brought Liam in for the sequel.

Man on the Move

Liam's future looks very bright. He and his *Hunger Games* costars were slated to film the sequel, *Catching Fire*, in 2012. November 2013 was the much-anticipated date of the film's opening. The third movie, *Mockingjay*, is also in the works.

Liam has definitely made his mark on America. And chances are, whatever he wants to do next with his career, a project (or two or three!) will be waiting for him.

A BITE OF 'MITE + LIAM = <3

Besides his parents and his friends, what does Liam miss from Australia? Vegemite—a dark brown veggie paste that you spread on crackers and bread. Yummers.

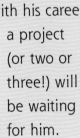

LIAM

PICS!

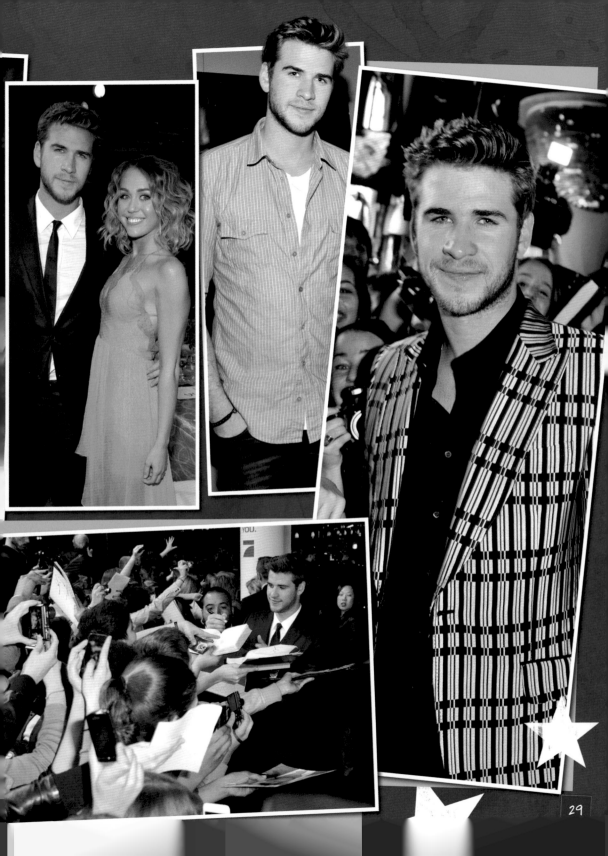

SOURCE NOTES

5   "*Hunger Games's*' Gale Talks to Fox 10," interview, FOX video, Phoenix, 7:52, March 7, 2012, http://www.myfoxphoenix.com/dpp/morning_show/hunger-games-gale-talks-to-fox-10-03072012 (June 13, 2012).

7   Ibid.

16–17   Caroline Gerrard, "Liam Hemsworth Interview for Teen and Tween Girls—Miss O & Friends," *Miss O & Friends*, March 21, 2012, http://www.missoandfriends.com/interviews/liam-hemsworth-interview.php (June 13, 2012).

18   Barbara Lynch, "Dreams Do Come True," *Townsville Bulletin*, April 1, 2010, http://www.townsvillebulletin.com.au/article/2010/04/01/127085_entertainment.html (June 13, 2012).

19   Ibid.

23   Jennifer Brett, "Liam Hemsworth Excited about *Hunger Games* Role," *AccessAtlanta*, March 21, 2012, http://www.accessatlanta.com/atlanta-movies/liam-hemsworth-excited-about-1388079.html?cxtype=rss_movies (June 13, 2012).

24   "*Hunger Games's* Gale Talks to Fox 10," interview.

25   Ibid.

MORE LIAM INFO

Collins, Suzanne. *The Hunger Games*. New York: Scholastic Press, 2008.
Read the novel that started it all.

IMDb: Liam Hemsworth
http://www.imdb.com/name/nm2955013
Visit the Internet Movie Database to find a listing of Liam's movies and TV credits, a brief biography, and articles about Liam.

Krohn, Katherine. *Jennifer Lawrence: Star of* The Hunger Games. Minneapolis: Lerner Publications Company, 2012.
Check out this in-depth biography of Jennifer Lawrence, which also includes plenty of deets on Liam and Josh.

Liam Hemsworth
http://www.liamhemsworth.bz
Find up-to-date pics and videos of Liam.

Liam Hemsworth Fans
http://liam-hemsworth.net
Check out this source for photos and news about Liam.

Williams, Mel. *Stars in the Arena: Meet the Hotties of* The Hunger Games. New York: Simon Pulse, 2012.
Read about Liam Hemsworth, Josh Hutcherson, and Jennifer Lawrence in this tell-all bio of the three celebs.

INDEX

Arabian Nights, 26
AWOL, 26

Blakelee, Will, 16
Branagh, Kenneth, 11, 14

Catching Fire, 27
Collins, Suzanne, 21
Cyrus, Miley, 15, 18, 25

engagement, 25
Expendables, The, 11, 27
Expendables 2, The, 27

Hawthorne, Gale, 21, 23
Hemsworth, Chris, 7, 13–14, 21
Hemsworth, Craig, 7, 9
Hemsworth, Leonie, 7, 9

Hemsworth, Luke, 7
Hunger Games, The, 5, 21–27
Hutcherson, Josh, 5, 22, 24

Knowing, 10–11

Last Song, The, 15–17, 19
Lawrence, Jennifer, 5, 22, 24

Mockingjay, 27

Ross, Gary, 21, 24

Sparks, Nicholas, 15
Stallone, Sylvester, 11, 27

Thor, 11, 13–14
Triangle, 10

The images in this book are used with the permission of: © George Pimentel/WireImage/Getty Images, pp. 2, 29 (right); © Serge Thomann/WireImage/Getty Images, pp. 3 (top), 9; © Sonia Recchia/WireImage/Getty Images, pp. 3 (bottom), 28 (top left); © Toby Canham/Getty Images, pp. 4 (top), 29 (top center); © Jesse Grant/Getty Images, p. 4 (bottom); AP Photo/Katy Winn, p. 5; Kathy Hutchins/Hutchins Photo/Newscom, p. 6 (top); © Tupungato/Dreamstime.com, p. 6 (bottom); © Colouria Media/Alamy, p. 7; © Pierre Tostee/ASP/Getty Images, p. 8; © First Look International/Courtesy Everett Collection, p. 10; © Eric Charbonneau/WireImage/Getty Images, pp. 12 (top), 21, 25 (top); Sam Emerson/© Walt Disney Studios Motion Pictures/Courtesy Everett Collection, p. 12 (bottom), 15, 16; PF 1 Wenn Photos/Newscom, p. 13; © Paramount Pictures/Courtesy Everett Collection, p. 14; Sinky/Macca/Splash News/Newscom, p. 17; © Jean Baptiste Lacroix/WireImage/Getty Images, p. 18; © Gregg DeGuire/FilmMagic/Getty Images, p. 19; © Dave Hogan/Getty Images, p. 20 (top); © Michael Buckner/Getty Images, p. 20 (bottom left); © Jason Merritt/Getty Images, p. 20 (bottom right); © s_buckley/Shutterstock.com, p. 22 (left); © Helga Esteb/Shutterstock.com, p. 22 (right); Murray Close/© Lionsgate/Courtesy Everett Collection, pp. 23, 24; © Splash News/CORBIS, p. 25 (bottom); © Joe Seer/Shutterstock.com, p. 26; Millennium Films/Newscom, p. 27; © Featureflash/Shutterstock.com, p. 28 (bottom left); © Taylor Hill/Film Magic/Getty Images, p. 28 (right); © Charley Gallay/Getty Images, p. 29 (top left); Picture Perfect/Rex USA, p. 29 (bottom left).

Front cover: © Jesse Grant/Getty Images (left); © Target Presse Agentur Gmbh/WireImage/Getty Images (right).

Back cover: © Jason Merritt/Getty Images.

Main body text set in Shannon Std Book 12/18.
Typeface provided by Monotype Typography.